# BRICK
## BUY BRICK

## DISTRESSED PROPERTY INVESTMENT

Matador
9 Priory Business Park,
Wistow Road, Kibworth Beauchamp,
Leicestershire. LE8 0RX
Tel: (+44) 116 279 2299
Fax: (+44) 116 279 2277
Email: books@troubador.co.uk
Web: www.troubador.co.uk/matador

ISBN 978 1783064 298

British Library Cataloguing in Publication Data.
A catalogue record for this book is available from the British Library.

Typeset by Troubador Publishing Ltd, Leicester, UK
Printed and bound in the UK by TJ International, Padstow, Cornwall

**Matador** is an imprint of Troubador Publishing Ltd

MIX
Paper from
responsible sources
FSC
www.fsc.org
FSC® C013056

# INTRODUCTION

This book in the Brick Buy Brick educational series has been written in association with Tigrent Learning UK, the UK's most respected provider of professional training programmes.

Tigrent and its associated network of industry experts and partners have a wealth of property investing knowledge. Tigrent trainers and customers derive from all ages and backgrounds and have over a decade's experience of working with new and existing investors from all over the world.

This book in the Brick Buy Brick series looks at distressed property and the opportunities it offers to the investor. Distressed property is all about adding value or buying below market value. Ideally

you will do both! The creative strategies explored in this book can enable you to advance way beyond the parameters of the average property investor. We explain how to make distressed property work for you, helping to open your eyes to the potential that is available and giving you that vital edge when investing.

For more information and to give us any feedback on your reading experience please visit

www.brick-buy-brick.co.uk.

# CHAPTER ONE

## STRATEGY EQUALS RESULTS

The number one requirement when investing is having the right mindset. Your property success rests on convincing people to sell their properties at the price that works for you. You also want people to lend money to you, partner with you, and work with you as part of your power team. Believing in yourself is key to success with others!

Adopt an aggressive buying strategy. Be creative – if you do the same as everyone else you will find there is more competition for the deals.

Develop clarity and vision. Know where you want to

be in five years time, in three years, next year... Take massive action. By this we mean do something that you are not doing right now – change your approach. It is through action that you acquire knowledge. Finally – get educated and stay close to other positive, like-minded people.

So, let's get started with distressed property. You can find it at all points in the spectrum, ranging from inexpensive (£0-£150k), mid-range (£150k-£500k) to large projects (£500k plus).

A low-end distressed property might be a standard terrace or semi in poor decorative order and perhaps with minor construction flaws. It should be in an area of high rental demand and provide a good yield. If you are looking to flip, ie buy, do up and sell on, the property should generate at least £10k profit when refurbished. The benefits of low-end properties are that they generate cash flow and improve your financial profile. They may well provide you with a model that can be repeated. For example, you buy a run-down two bed terrace in an area where three beds are in high rental demand. By reconfiguring the layout you create three bedrooms, thereby adding value. You refurbish and the house rents out easily. If there are enough similar terraces in the area you can repeat the process, buying and refurbishing along the same lines. These properties then give you the cash flow that enables you to build a solid base to your portfolio.

The disadvantages of cheaper properties are that they can take up time and money managing tenants, voids and repairs.

Your strategies for sourcing low-end property may be to buy them yourself or from an investor or sourcing agent. The key when buying yourself is to get as close as possible to the vendor. You can find investors by networking. Ask estate and letting agents if they know any landlords who are selling off their portfolios. Do your research well and see what is selling or renting the fastest in the area. Have a full understanding of the type of tenants you

are targeting and what they require. Analyse where the highest rental demand is and satisfy that, whether it is 3 bed semis or 1 bed flats. Don't just buy a property, cross your fingers and hope someone will rent it – do your homework!

Sourcing agents may be local or national. Local agents know the area and may provide a shortcut to deals and to a local power team. Find them at networking meetings, online forums or through letting agents. National agents cover large areas and offer many leads. Find them in investment magazines, through local or national newspapers or online.

If you use a sourcing agent double check the information, visit properties, check their rental history. Look for any damage and calculate the cost of repairs. Get valuations, research the market. While using a sourcing agent saves time, your offer has to take their fees into account.

Middle range properties can give you better cash

4

flow and also asset appreciation. On the downside yields tend to be lower, they are more expensive to refurbish and if you rent them out you also have to deal with management and repairs.

Large projects, such as converting a nursing home into an HMO or an office block into flats, have potential for the most forced appreciation and for the highest yields. For your first project at this level you might consider using a company who will help you get planning approval, help with the design project, and liaise with building control in return for a fee or a percentage of the deal.

In the next chapter we look at sourcing distressed property in more detail. Remember – whichever strategy you use, perseverance is the hard work you do after you get tired of doing the hard work you already did! Your best deal will be the one you put the most effort into.

# CHAPTER TWO

## BUYING DISTRESSED PROPERTY

When sourcing distressed property yourself use different strategies to get leads flowing your way. Bear in mind that some of the best deals come from places where other investors lack the know-how to go. You can buy from national agents, local agents, direct from the developer, direct from the vendor, or from auction. There are also websites dedicated to distressed property, such as www.pickupaproperty.com.

*Direct marketing*

Try to access properties before they hit the internet sites by marketing direct to owners who are willing to sell at a discount. These may be going through divorce, hardship, repossession, or perhaps they have more positive lifestyle reasons such as emigration or moving in with a partner. When marketing it is a good idea to use a dedicated phone that is different from your personal phone.

*Advertise*

Place a goldmine ad in the local press. This can be as simple as 'I buy houses fast' with a name and number.

Drop leaflets. They should be A5 and double-sided. Make them look different. Have a compelling message. Leaflets should target a specific area such as a cluster of streets. You may have to arrange repeated drops in order to get a response.
Advertise on the side of your car (a car wrap).

*Websites*

Create your own website stating what you're looking for. Make sure the content is interesting and stresses

the benefits of what you are offering. Again, think about what a distressed seller needs: 'I can help you sell your home fast,' or 'sell your house fast for cash.' Get someone to do the SEO properly. Tip: Put a local number on your site and pay an answering service. This also helps search engines.

*Empty homes*

Search for these by driving the streets, or even better, walking them. Knock on doors, talk to neighbours, talk to the local authority's empty homes officer. Check the land registry. If a property is empty for more than six months the local authority can take control of it for seven years, refurbish it and let to DSS tenants before handing the owner a repair bill. They do this using an Empty Dwelling Management Order (EDMO). If you find the owner of the property you have a bargaining tool by pointing out that they are exposing themselves to an EDMO. Tip: look for local authority grants or loans to help bring the property back into use.

When potential vendors call ask how you can help. Assure them that any information they give you is confidential. Draw up a fact-finder list of questions beforehand and run through these. Ask for the property's address, a full description of it and its condition. You also need to know the vendor's financial situation. Take their name and ask for the number they want to be phoned back on. At the end of the initial conversation tell them that you will call back within a certain amount of time, such as 24 hours. Stick to this. If you don't, they will move on to the next advertiser.

Now assess the opportunity. Look at the area; work out a maximum likely purchase price. Think about the property's potential for added value. Can you extend it, put in a loft, parcel off the garden? Will it rent? Talk to local agents. If you think the property has potential call back and make an initial conditional offer. If they agree then arrange a visit. You need to assess the property and its condition. By making the effort to visit and build a rapport with the vendor you gain an edge over your competitors. Before you visit enquire how many people are on the title deeds and ask for them all to be present. When you arrive put the vendor/s at their ease. Discuss the situation and why they want to sell. Perhaps they are facing repossession. In the next chapter we discuss this situation and the measures you need to take to stop it going through.

When you negotiate with the vendor ask them how close they can come to your offer. This keeps the focus on the price you want to bring them to. Be prepared to walk away if you can't reach an agreement, but before you do so give them your card and ask if it will be okay to give them a call in a month's time. Call in a week.

Be professional. Once you agree on a price stick to it unless there is good reason to change it, such as the results of a structural survey.

*Auctions*

These are a great source of distressed properties. Auctions tend to scare off the average investor so this cuts down the competition. You may get a fantastic deal and you know it's yours once the hammer goes down. You can buy before the auction, in the room, or afterwards if it doesn't sell. Sites such as www.propertyauctionaction.co.uk list forthcoming auctions. You can register with individual auction houses and they will send their catalogues either online or by post.

Property goes to auction for a variety of reasons, such as probate sales, bank repossessions and empty council stock. It may be a property with serious structural problems or be highly unusual – lighthouses and nuclear bunkers have made appearances in auction rooms!

Be careful to read the conditions of sale. What exactly is being sold – does the building come with the land? Is there a sitting tenant? Is it in an area of mining or flooding? You should pre-order the legal pack and have your solicitor read through it.

There are set times and dates when you can view

properties before an auction. Try to get to the first viewing in case you need to return. You can take your valuer and/or builder with you. Have a survey or valuation done prior to the auction.

If you think you can add enough value to the property you might offer over the guide price before the auction. If your offer is accepted you may be required to exchange in 28 days or before the auction date.

Note that the guide price is the value the auctioneer expects the property to fetch – in theory – but it is often set low in order to attract potential bidders through the door. Properties often sell for substantially more than the guide price. The reserve price is the value below which the vendor will not sell.

Pick your spot in the room – it is best to stand at the back so you can see who else is bidding. Know the maximum price you are prepared to pay and if the bidding goes above this, walk away. There is another deal around the corner.

The fall of the auctioneer's hammer is a contract between two parties. The vendor and buyer sign a memorandum of sale to make the purchase binding. The auctioneer can sign on behalf of both or either party. The standard deposit is usually 10%, payable on the day of auction. If you don't complete in 28 days you will be liable for interest. Always remember to have your finances in place when bidding. Not all lenders act quickly. In case of delay you can arrange bridging, but make sure you factor in the cost of this. As soon as you buy the property call your broker to insure it.

If a property fails to sell at auction you may make an offer on it afterwards. Check auction house results lists. If the property failed to reach the reserve price you have scope for negotiation. You may also get more flexible payment terms.

*Liquidators*

These manage and sell off portfolios as a step before repossession by commercial lenders. If you are in a

position to buy several properties at once you can approach the liquidator and make a pre-auction offer. When talking to them present yourself as a property company and prove that you have the funds to buy several properties. You will need a firm of solicitors with more than three partners to handle the transaction.

# CHAPTER THREE

## REPOSSESSIONS

Vendors facing repossessions are highly motivated and your ability to move quickly to remedy their situation provides an opportunity to achieve a below market value discount.

Repossessions are usually brought by first chargees, but increasingly by second chargees. After a few missed payments the chargees (the banks etc) will write to the owner to arrange a payment plan. If the owner fails to respond or does not keep up with their payment plan the lender will apply to the County Court for possession and a hearing date will be set. Up to that stage if the homeowner gets a sale on the open market the repossession is stopped.

Judges normally work hard to stop repossession. If the owner offers to clear the arrears over an agreed period a suspended possession order is made. But if the owner fails to turn up in court or to pay the order agreement, the lender will be granted a possession order or warrant. This is an eviction by bailiffs and the ultimate deadline for the owner to leave.

When approached by a vendor facing repossession you need to empathise – they are in a crisis. Build a rapport with them. Reassure them you can probably help and in order to do so you need to ask some questions. Do a complete fact-find. Gather as much financial information and copies of paperwork as you can. For a small fee the Land Registry will tell you how many loans are secured against the property. Obtain reliable figures by contacting lenders who have money secured against the property – the homeowner has to give you third party authorisation to speak to each lender. Also find out if the vendor has any unsecured debt. If after doing your research, you decide you don't want to buy the property you can always source it on. You can also suggest that the vendor contacts Citizens Advice, talks to the lender and attends the court hearing, but never give financial advice – you are not regulated.

Let's say you want to buy the property and the vendor accepts your offer, but an eviction has already been booked. You can still act to stop it taking place. Get the vendor to apply to the county court for an emergency hearing on the basis of solicitors being instructed on the sale of the house on the open market. You do this by downloading an N244 form from www.hmcourts-service.gov.uk Help the vendor fill in the form, which is simply an application for an emergency court hearing, and then submit it to the court.

Contact your solicitor and broker. Book a survey if you need one. Move quickly! Have your power team in place. Include a repossession specialist lawyer on your power team. These can liaise with lenders, submit applications to court and instruct solicitors to attend hearings. Use solicitors who can exchange and complete fast. If you have a pending possession order deadline or bailiff's eviction get your solicitor to seek a stay of execution from the lenders.

In building up a business that acquires property through stopping repossessions you have to be able to deal with the emotional side. Always be diplomatic. Reassure the vendor. A confident approach will put them at their ease. Remember — they expect you to ask financial questions so don't be embarrassed.

# CHAPTER FOUR

## BRIDGING AND COMMERCIAL FINANCE

Some distressed property strategies require commercial finance as there are restrictions on normal buy to let loans. You will need this type of finance for example, if you want to buy a shop with a flat above it. Commercial lending also applies to residential investments such as breaking up a large office to turn into flats or an HMO. There is also development lending for projects such as loft conversions.

Commercial lending comes mainly from private investment banks and also some High Street banks such as Lloyds. Most will lend on minimum valuations of £100,000. Some will lend interest only. Interest rates vary from around 4.5% to 14% over base (at the time of writing), so get a good broker. Over 70% LTV, rates can get very high. The loan is usually, but not always, for 5 years.

Commercial valuations are different from normal buy to lets. In the case of a shop with a flat above it, the valuation for the shop will be ten times the rental income, while the flat's valuation will be based on comparables. Both valuations will be rolled into the loan.

Some lenders like HMOs, some like student lets, and none like social housing. They usually want to know that you already have buy to let experience. The area you are investing in will be important to them.

You may need commercial lending if you buy a property that has been split into flats under one title. Commercial lending can also apply once you have a portfolio of eight or nine properties. At this stage the normal buy to let lenders consider you to be overexposed so they may only offer 50% LTV. A commercial lender views portfolio finance as spreading the risk. When applying for a loan seek advice from an accountant or tax advisor on whether you need to be a limited company or not.

Bridging finance is also a type of commercial lending. Basically it is a short-term loan secured on a property. It can be very useful if, for example, you are buying a shop to convert into a flat and need to apply for change of use and planning or you are buying at auction and need to move quickly.

Another use for bridging is when you find a property that is too distressed for a conventional buy to let mortgage. Let's say the kitchen has been ripped out and the toilet smashed. Buy to let mortgages stipulate that the property must be 'habitable' ie have a useable kitchen and bathroom. There are both light and heavy refurb bridges available that can be really useful in these circumstances. Be aware that lenders like you to put some of your own money into the work.

When applying for bridging finance you will need to answer five basic questions. What is the reason for the bridge, how much do you want, what security are you offering, how will the interest be serviced and what is your intended exit? The lender will also want to know where you are buying. Explain the sum you are expecting to pay for the property, the sum you expect to spend on refurbishment, and your anticipated revaluation figure. You are also likely to need a valuation report and a schedule of works.

When purchasing the property calculate the cost of the bridging so that you can factor this into your offer. There are three interest payment options; monthly payments, interest rolled up into the redemption payment so that you are paying compound interest, or all the interest may be deducted in advance from the loan.

If you want the bridging in order to buy, refurb and sell on, it is vital to remember the buy to let six-month rule. If your buyer is purchasing the property with a mortgage, you have to wait six months from the day when you complete to the day when you sell (this does not of course apply if you have a cash buyer).

Let's say you bridge the purchase price and the cost of refurbishment for, say, eight months and you know the refurbishment will only take three months. In this case it makes sense to borrow the refurbishment costs after the third month. This allows you to do the work and sell in six months, factoring in a further two months for the sale to go through. Some bridging companies want to inspect the refurbishment work before they will release the next tranche of money. When applying for your loan it is a good idea to say that you want it for longer than you think you need in order to save going into default. If you do not repay the loan in the agreed time then interest rates can go as high as 5% a month.

Traditionally, lenders give you around 70% of the value of the property but this may vary considerably according to area. Bridging interest rates are usually around 1% to 1.25% (1.45% for development loans) per month with a 2% arrangement fee. Loan to value varies between 60% and 80%.

Always use a reputable broker – get recommendations. Your broker will usually charge 1% to 2% of the total. He or she will want your complete financial background: ID, credit report, at least three months original statements for all your bank statements. You and your broker should also be confident of your exit strategy.

Make sure you have a solicitor who has experience of dealing with transactions that involve bridging and commercial finance.

Refinancing from a bridge to a commercial loan can take a few months to arrange. It is crucial to note that lenders will allow you to borrow up to 90% of the *purchase price* and up to 90% of the works, (subject to 75% LTV) for the first 12 months. This means you have to wait a year before you can get a loan based on the value of the renovated property. If you have bridged in order to do up a property that would qualify for normal buy to let lending then you only have to wait for six months.

It may seem expensive but bridging can be a very useful tool for building your portfolio. Potentially there are no limits to the number of loans you can have and they are usually arranged quickly. This is important – it is often the buyer who can move the fastest who gets the best deal. The obvious disadvantage is that bridging costs more, but then again you are not buying these types of property at full market price. Factor the cost into your budget when you make your offer.

To sum up, think of bridging and commercial finance as a problem-solving tool. This sort of lending is flexible – it is not FSA regulated – and it gives you access to deals which potentially have more money to be made in them.

# CHAPTER FIVE

## SURVEYING PROPERTY

When viewing a property you need to identify any structural or surface defects and calculate the cost of putting these right. If you need to investigate further, for example if there are signs of serious structural problems such as cracking in the brickwork, then call in a specialist.

*Externally*

First examine the outside of the property. Note any points of concern so that you can check the corresponding internal area. The two most serious issues are water ingress and structural problems.

 DISTRESSED PROPERTY INVESTMENT

Water can enter from the roof, walls or ground and can in itself be a cause of structural instability.

Start from the top — it helps to bring a pair of binoculars to check the roof. Examine the chimney pots, the stack and the lead work that seals the chimney to the roof (flashings). Are any slates or tiles missing from the roof? Has the property been extended? Once inside, view the roof of a single storey extension from an upper floor window. If it has a flat roof look for standing water, cracking or blistering. If it's a double storey extension, then check the ceiling from inside.

Look at the alignment of the gutters — do they overflow? Can you see stains on the surface of the walls? Cast iron downpipes may become corroded. Insert your hand between them and the wall to feel for any roughness.

Check the brickwork. Make sure the mortar (pointing) is in good condition so that water cannot seep through and cause problems within the property. Be careful with properties of non-standard construction, such as post-war housing with concrete walls which often have damp issues. Also look for deflected lintels and cracks in the brickwork. Stand next to the walls and look along them for bulging. If the property is rendered check for cracks. Render should not go right down to the ground but have a metal trim around the bottom in order not to breach any damp course.

Are there any trees growing close to the house? Roots can cause a problem with foundations. Watch for Japanese knot weed which can grow through tarmac and concrete. Check boundary walls are intact and in place.

*Internally*

Look for stains and mould on the walls. Mould in one spot could just be a result of condensation and may be cleaned off. If it has spread then there might be a damp problem. If the property has no damp proof course (DPC) water may rise up to a metre above the floor, rot floor timbers, ruin decoration and create a health hazard. Tip: Check for rot by stamping on the edge of floors to see if they give.

Even if a damp proof course has been put in it may have failed. Buy a damp meter and run it around the walls and floors. If there are signs of damp, call in a specialist. Some companies charge for a survey but they will take the cost off any works carried out. DPCs should be guaranteed for 20 to 25 years. Make sure air bricks are not blocked.

There are two types of timber rot: wet and dry. It is important to distinguish these. Wet rot often comes from a leaking gutter and does not spread. Dry rot is a fungus that attacks timber and spreads – it can move 3m a year! It can even go through brickwork and concrete. To treat it you have to cut away the timber for a metre around the affected area and treat with fungicide. Dry rot spores are in the air all the time and need ventilation to disperse them. This is why air bricks are so important. Dry rot has a smell rather like mouldy cheese and begins with a

brown fruiting body. These often grow in cupboards or cellars so always look in these when viewing. Check the floor by bouncing lightly. Does it spring? This can be – but is not necessarily – a symptom of dry rot and you will need to investigate further.

Check joists and skirting. Look for woodworm holes. If you see these then have the woodwork looked at by an expert. It may need replacing or simply treating with insecticide.

Try to check the roof from inside by looking through the loft hatch. Is there any daylight coming through? Turn on your torch and examine the roof timbers. Are there any water stains on the rafters or purlins?

It may be hard to spot problems with bay window roofs. Look at their ceilings from inside. Is there staining? Has the lintel above the bay window bowed? It can be expensive to put in a new lintel and brickwork.

Are there gaps behind or below the skirting boards?

Do the floors bow or slope? Do the doors shut properly? If you suspect structural movement then you need to investigate further. It could be old movement, for example, a one-off event such as a bomb falling nearby during the war. Has there been mining in the area? If you have any concerns you need to call in a structural surveyor.

Movement can be remedied by underpinning the walls. This means digging down a metre or more and pumping in concrete and is expensive. If there are severe cracks in the wall (look to see whether the cracks actually cut through the bricks rather than following their line) the whole wall may need to be rebuilt, which is likely to cost tens of thousands of pounds.

Are all the internal walls in place? If reconfiguration has been carried out, for example if the ground floor has been made open plan, make sure the floors above are correctly supported. Bounce on the upstairs floor to check for movement. Is there cracking on the walls? Where structural work has

been done ask to see the completion certificate.

Check the electrics. If there are surface cables on the kitchen walls, surface fixed sockets and a fuse box with no breaker switches you will be looking to do full or partial rewiring.

Check plumbing, sanitary fittings, gas appliances and pipework. Where there is a cold water storage tank under the roof you would normally remove this and put in a combi boiler.

Asbestos is now illegal in the UK. In residential properties there may be asbestos in Artex. As long as it remains intact you may paint or plaster over it, but if you want to remove it call in a specialist. You might find asbestos cement roofing sheets in outbuildings and garages. If you take these down they have to go to a licensed tip; if they are damaged you need to call in a licensed asbestos contractor to remove them.

Basically, if the property is seriously distressed have

a full structural report carried out. When it comes to surveying, remember that the more information you gather the greater your clarity on costs and the stronger your negotiating position when buying.

# CHAPTER SIX

## PROJECT MANAGEMENT

You are creating something that people want to live in. While this is both exciting and rewarding, it is crucial to get right. First of all research your area and decide on your exit strategy. Know the sales and rental market inside out. What types of properties are in demand? What amenities do people want? Find out the average income in the area. What jobs do people have? Will you sell or rent out the property when it's done up? If rental, who to? A family let or an HMO? Know your target market – students, LHA, key workers, families or professionals.

If you are thinking of extending the property find out the ceiling prices in the area and balance these against the cost of works. Check demand. There is no point extending to make your property a 4 bed house if the demand in the area is primarily for 2 beds. It might be a good idea to start with £10,000-£12,000 refurbs where there is a low level of risk. Understanding the process at this level will help you expand to larger and more complex projects with higher returns.

If you want to extend get council approval before you start. Planning permission can in itself add a lot of value. Know your market well so that you have a good idea of what the council will allow. Planning can take between two months and a year to come through, so budget for the cost of this.

Prepare for the renovation process. Allow for the time to manage it yourself or leverage someone else's time. Get the right people to do the job. Hire a reputable builder. Get recommendations. View their previous work. Are they open and easy to

communicate with? Could you work with them?
Trust your gut feeling. Choose a builder who is proud
of their work. Tip: look at the condition of the
vehicle they arrive in. If it's a rust-bucket with graffiti
written in the dust on its sides warning bells should
start to ring.

Decide whether you or the builder will be project
manager. Who will buy materials? If you are buying
them yourself you can get substantial discounts by
opening trade accounts with big suppliers such as
Howdens. You may need to form a limited company
to qualify but this can be cheaply and simply done
online.

Walk through the property with the builder so that
they understand the work you want to have done.
Set a budget and get three quotes. Make sure it's a
quote, ie a fixed price, and not an estimate. Agree a
rate for unforeseen extra work so that there are no
nasty surprises. Agree a schedule of works, a
payment plan and a time frame. Check your builder's
insurance. Hold back 20% to be paid after any

defects in the work (snagging) are taken care of.

When it comes to refurbishments don't over or under spend. The key is to keep emotion out of it and not get carried away with your own artistic ideas. You are not going to live in the place yourself! Find out what local standards and tastes are and stick to these. Your builder should be able to guide you here.

When doing a refurb it is crucial that you understand where your money is going. Draw up a spreadsheet, go through the property room by room, itemising what is needed, the quantity, material and labour costs.

The importance of the spreadsheet is that it will give you clarity about what you are spending so that you know your costs in advance. It may take a while to draw up for your first project but it is an invaluable model to use as you build up your portfolio.

While you want your builder to make money on the project, you also want to know where your money is going. If it is a small job, let the builder quote a lump sum, but on higher end projects give them a copy of your spreadsheet and let them fill it in.

Sign a contract with the builder, make sure you pay on time and motivate them by finding another house nearby which you will want them to do up when they have finished the present job.

*The building process*

First, there will be a strip out for which you need to hire skips. This is followed by first fix, which includes addressing any structural issues, plastering, screeding the floors, electrics, a damp proof course if necessary, fixing the roofs and gutters and treating any dry rot. Also to be considered are plumbing for the kitchen, bathroom and radiators.

The second fix consists of decorating, tiling, putting in the kitchen, radiators, and flooring. Then there is the final clean up and lastly you need to go through the property with the builder to look for snagging.

Keep an eye on the work as it progresses. Turn up unannounced and see how the builder is getting on. You can advertise the property before the work is finished, taking photos as different areas are completed.

*Finishing*

Create a schedule of finishes. If the builder knows the local market let them choose the fixtures and fittings. If it is a higher end or more complex project you should select these yourself, or perhaps engage an interior designer to do this. Finally you may want to dress the property in order for it to rent or sell more easily.

# CHAPTER SEVEN

## PROPERTY DESIGN AND STAGING

With mid to high end properties you might want to include a designer, an architect and structural engineer on your team.

You will need an architect to draw up plans if you intend to extend. Architects bring vision and experience and can help you maximise the value of your property. Allow around 8 to 10% on top of your build costs for their fee.

In areas such as London where you might struggle to buy below market value you can look to add a huge amount of value by extending. Remember to factor in enough time for planning permission. Make sure you know the tenure of your property before you extend. If it is leasehold you will have to get the permission of the freeholder. Basically you can build up, down or sideways. Weigh up your costs. In some areas basement extensions are very popular, for example. These can add a lot of value but are generally very expensive to do.

Tip: have a look on Google Maps to see what neighbours have done at the back of their properties.

Can you visualise the finished product before you start the renovation process? If you struggle with this, you may want to hire an interior designer. Again, balance the cost against the benefits. A designer can save you time running around and also help you maximise the value of the property. Remember – if you use an interior designer, don't get carried away! Make sure you keep to a very strict budget.

When it comes to buying a house it is women who are usually the main decision-makers. Think about the quality of the kitchen and bathroom. Don't cut corners here – it pays to install a good quality shower, for example. Focus on areas the buyer or tenant will touch the most, such as door handles or light switches. If you upgrade these you will add instant value. Tip: although they only cost a few pounds, satin chrome switches look expensive.

Choose neutral colours that don't date. It is better to use good quality paint that will last longer, saving on redecoration costs. Repeat colour schemes and concepts. In cheaper areas gain the edge by studying competitors' products and making yours that little bit better.

Curtains date and can look drab; it is better to invest in white roller blinds or timber venetians. Pick at least one fancy light. Shop around for good quality appliances at bargain prices. Tip: try www.applianceworldonline.com. Make sure your appliance warranty extends for more than 12 months.

It is best to lay tiles on kitchens and bathroom floors but you may want to use vinyl in the cheapest properties. Choose good-quality neutral colour carpets; in cheaper properties you might choose a wool/nylon blend.

Whether it is a high or low-end property don't overlook the finishing touches. You want to make people feel that they can move in straight away.

Dress the finished house or flat with furniture and accessories, reusing these as you buy more properties. Dressed properties rent or sell faster as they enable people to visualise where their furniture will go. If your property is an HMO dress one or two rooms. If you don't want to buy furniture for this purpose you can hire it. When choosing furniture or accessories it's a good idea to select classic designs in neutral shades with one or two accent colours.

Remember when you hold an open house appeal to all the senses. Put fresh flowers on display and light scented candles. You could even percolate coffee.

First impressions are important! To sum up, when designing and staging your property be creative, stick to your budget, spend your time wisely and have fun!

# CHAPTER EIGHT

## MAKING IT A BUSINESS

Make sure you regard property investment as a business – if you don't, then basically you have a nice hobby. Put your systems in place. First of all get advice on structure. Will you operate as an individual or a limited company? Put your power team together. Consider all your funding options. Raise private money. Prepare documents that you can present to potential investors/angels/joint venture partner/friends and family.

Target specific areas. If your area is full of other investors then change your strategy or change area. If you go for properties that everyone can fund then there may be too much competition. Be creative – use commercial finance and find new ways to add value. Remember that tax efficiency is vital – for this kind of investment it is important you talk to an advisor who understands your strategy.

Research properties and conduct feasibility studies on them. Decide what you will offer and learn to negotiate. Negotiation is where you make the money. Sound confident!

Draw up a spreadsheet so you understand the cost of renovations. Decide on your exit – whether you will sell on or rent out, and if so, who your tenants will be.

The biggest hurdle in investing is the fear factor and that is overcome by going out and taking action! Don't wait for conditions to be perfect before you start. If something goes wrong then remind yourself that you wouldn't be in that position if you weren't trying. Remember – there are no mistakes except those we fail to learn from.

Adopt the traits of a successful person. Feed yourself with positive messages. If you don't understand something or don't know how to do it – get educated.

Choose a strategy that excites you, that gets you out of bed at 4 am. Finally – remember to adopt the right attitude: dream; dare; determine; do!

# CHAPTER NINE

## BRIDGING CASE STUDIES

Here we give a couple of real-life examples that show the calculations you need to do to see whether or not there will be a large enough profit in a deal for bridging to work for you.

*Case Study One*

You are buying a two bedroom flat in South London that needs full redecoration and modernisation. It is too distressed to be mortgageable. You need to calculate bridging costs so that you can see whether the deal works.

 DISTRESSED PROPERTY INVESTMENT

| | |
|---|---|
| Asking price | £239, 950 |
| Accepted offer | £210,000 |
| Bridging costs (7 months) | £33,186 |
| Stamp duty @ 1% | £2,100 |
| Refurb costs | £31,550 |
| Legals | £1,000 |
| Total spend | £277, 836 |

You expect the works to take five months and to save on interest payments you will borrow the refurb costs in month 2. If you bridge the costs of the purchase price of £210,000 and the refurb costs of £31,550 @ 2% the monthly interest rates break down as follows:

Month 1 interest £4,200

Month 2 interest £4831 (£210,000 + £31,500 = £241,550 @ 2 %)

£4831 paid each month for six months = £28,986

Total bridging for seven months £33,186 (£28,986 + £4200)

You expect a done up valuation of £315,000

Selling the property on at £310,000, with legals of £1,000, agent fees @ 2% of £6,200 you would give you £302,800

£302,800 – £277,836 gives you a profit of £24,964

*Case Study Two*

You are carrying out a feasibility study on a property in Hull. It is a 3 bedroom, 3 reception house on a pleasant street near the city centre with a hospital at one end. It needs a full refurb.

| | |
|---|---|
| Asking price: | £85,000 |
| Refurb costs: | £38,000 |
| Total | £123,000 |
| Valued at | £160,000 |

Consider your exit strategies. Will you rent out to a family or as an HMO? Or will you refurb and sell?

Looking at the figures it is clear that buying the property at asking price would leave £3,000 in the deal (remortgaging at 75% LTV)

In this case the buyer negotiated the purchase price down to £55,000. In its current state the property was unmortgageable so he used £11,000 from savings and bridged £44,000 (80% LTV) and the £38,000 refurb costs.

The works would take 3 months to complete, but because of the 6 month rule he decided not to start until month 4, in order to save on bridging costs. He would borrow the £38,000 in three stages of £12,667 each. An extra 2 months were factored in to allow for the investor's purchase process.

Bridging £44,000 at 1.5% interest he paid the following:

Month 1 £660

Month 2 £660

Month 3 £660

On Month 4 he borrowed the first amount of

£12,667, meaning he paid £850 interest (£44,000 +
£12,667 = £56,667 @ 1.5%)
Month 5 £1040 (£56,667 + £12,667 = £69,334 @ 1.5%)
Month 6 £1230 (£69,334 + £12666 = £82,000 @ 1.5%)
Month 7 £1230
Month 8 £1230
The total cost of bridging for 8 months was £7,560

The buyer paid in total:

| | |
|---|---|
| Purchase price | £55,000 |
| Refurb costs | £38,000 |
| Bridging costs | £7,560 |
| Legal fees | £1,000 |
| Total | £101,560 |

In this instance the buyer decided to sell at 75% of
market value to another investor who was planning
to rent out the property as an HMO for nurses.
The full market value was £160,000
£160,000@75% = £120,000

This gave him a profit £18,440 (£120,000 – £101,560)

The buyer had other exit strategies. If he had decided to sell on the open market he could have made a larger profit. In this case he wanted to sell quickly in order to move on to the next deal.

# CHAPTER TEN

## CASE STUDY – DREW AND ANNA PEARCE

Investing in distressed property has transformed the lives of Drew and Anna Pearce. Three years ago they were struggling financially. By late 2010 Drew, who has a background in management, had been out of work for several months. Anna, an actuary, was also facing redundancy. Their rent was £1,000 a month and they had thousands of pounds of consumer debt. "We thought – what are we going to do if Anna loses her job? How will we repay our debts?"

They noticed a property exhibition was being held nearby and decided to go. "Only because it would be a nice day out and we might even get a cup of tea!" At the exhibition they were invited to a seminar run by Tigrent on how to invest in property. "Again we went because it was free!" But the information presented inspired them to sign up for a training course. "We put the cost on a credit card. It was scary, we discussed it for a long time, but by then we realised the only thing that was stopping us from being financially free was ourselves. What we had been doing up till then wasn't working – and so we took a big leap of faith."

The first thing Drew and Anna were taught was how to clarify their goals. They worked out that in the next 12 months they could clear their debts of £45,000 by flipping three properties. In the following year they would work towards their freedom figure of £3,000 passive income per month.

They found an area in the Midlands that fitted their strategy and worked very hard researching, viewing and talking to estate agents. One of their offers was quickly accepted. "But we had no money! We didn't know how we'd actually buy the property." They contacted their trainer who gave them advice on how to structure a proposal to potential investors. This enabled them to raise the finances for the 25% deposit and refurb.

And then Anna lost her job. This motivated the couple even more. They refurbished their first property and sold it to a first time buyer. "It only needed cosmetic work. We made £10,000 profit – that was £3,000 more than we had budgeted for!"

Soon after this they had two more offers accepted. "The second property was a full refurb. By the time we'd finished it we'd done our distressed property training and we knew how to add value. We dressed it for viewings and priced it a little below others in the street. Ours sold the quickest as we'd been shown how to present it properly."

They made £19,000 profit on this second property – £9,000 more than the first – which they say is a clear financial indicator of the benefits of training.

"We did what we were shown – we were too scared to deviate from what we had been taught because the cost of mistakes can be high!"

In less than a year agents were giving Drew and Anna first calls before advertising properties on the market. "They knew what we were looking for and that no matter how smelly the property was, unlike some other buyers we would be happy to view it."

The couple, who are in their thirties, admit that first year was tough. They worked exceptionally hard and made sacrifices, even moving back in with Anna's mum for a while. But in a year they had repaid their debts and covered the cost of their training. After that things changed quickly for them. They bought a small distressed property for themselves, did it up and moved in. They got married and then Anna found she was pregnant. "That was a bit sooner than planned so we started to look around for a 3 bedroom house."

In less than three years Anna and Drew have created

a position for themselves where they don't need to work unless they choose to. Nowadays they both enjoy having the time to look after baby Louise while running their property business. They continue to focus on distressed property because it works for them.

"Everything we buy is distressed. We know what we are looking for now and our profits have risen steadily as we have done more training."

Anna and Drew would advise anyone embarking on a property journey not to worry too much about finances but just get out there and start investing. "If you are looking to take control of your life then the help is there for you. With the right education property investing can totally change your life."

The couple are proof positive of this!

# CHAPTER ELEVEN

## CONCLUSION

This introduction to Distressed Property is designed to help the investor understand the potential benefits of buying for forced appreciation. The key here is to know how to source these types of property, how to negotiate for them and how to access the appropriate finance. Having acquired your property you need to understand what the renovation process entails and how to manage it. Arming yourself with these tools will put you ahead of the field, in a position to build a strong investment portfolio. While the scope is virtually limitless it is a good idea to start on smaller, low risk projects and build up the experience and confidence to go on to

the larger deals where there is more money to be made. We hope you enjoy the creativity, satisfaction and returns that come from investing in distressed property and we wish you the very best of luck on your Brick Buy Brick journey!

This book is part of the Brick Buy Brick series, created in association with Tigrent Learning Ltd, who have been at the forefront of UK investment training since 2002.

Copyright ©2014 Tigrent Learning UK Limited

www.brick-buy-brick.co.uk

# NOTES

# NOTES

**BRICK BUY BRICK** DISTRESSED PROPERTY INVESTMENT

# NOTES

# NOTES

# NOTES

# NOTES